CHI-HOON
A KOREAN GIRL

CHI-HOON
A KOREAN GIRL

by Patricia McMahon

With photographs by

Michael F. O'Brien

BOYDS MILLS PRESS

ACKNOWLEDGMENTS

❖   ❖   ❖

I find it difficult to frame a thank-you large enough to express my gratitude to Yu Young-nan, Kim Seung-kyung, Kim Chi-young, and, of course, Kim Chi-hoon for their kindness, generosity, hospitality, and forbearance in allowing Michael and me to disrupt their world. I want to thank Yu Young-nan especially for her translation, for all her insights, and for giving this imperfect person the gift of friendship. Kamsahamnida.

I offer my most sincere gratitude to Professor Edward W. Wagner of the Department of East Asian Languages and Culture at Harvard University for his generous gift of time and information. Sincere gratitude as well to Karen Klockner, my editor, who understood the idea.

There are so many fellow sojourners in Seoul whom I would like to name, had I pages to fill, but I must thank Kathy and David Allan for bed, board, transport, and more on the book expedition; Good Friends Dunks, who always help; Ruth and Nigel, who would have if they could, and Russell and Pat Proctor.

A very special thank-you, from both Michael O'Brien and myself, to the Honorable Donald Gregg, American Ambassador to Korea, and Margaret Gregg for their kind support and generous hospitality.

PUBLISHED BY CAROLINE HOUSE
BOYDS MILLS PRESS, INC.
A HIGHLIGHTS COMPANY
815 CHURCH STREET
HONESDALE, PENNSYLVANIA 18431
PRINTED IN MEXICO

Publisher Cataloging-in-Publication Data

McMahon, Patricia.
        Chi-hoon : a Korean girl / by Patricia McMahon ; with photographs
by Michael F. O'Brien. — 1st ed.
[48] p. : col. ill. ; cm.
Summary: The story of a young Korean girl, her family, and their life in Seoul, Korea.
ISBN 1-56397-026-0
1. Korea (South) —Juvenile literature. [1. Korea (South).]
951.95—dc20   1993
Library of Congress Catalog Card Number: 92-81331

FIRST EDITION, 1993
BOOK DESIGNED BY JEANNE ABBOUD
THE TEXT OF THIS BOOK IS SET IN 13.2-POINT SABON.
DISTRIBUTED BY ST. MARTIN'S PRESS

10 9 8 7 6 5 4

For Joseph McCarthy—
Companion on all the journeys

For Conor Clarke McCarthy—
My Small One, Seasoned Traveler

— P. M.

For Arline and for Sean

— M. F. O.

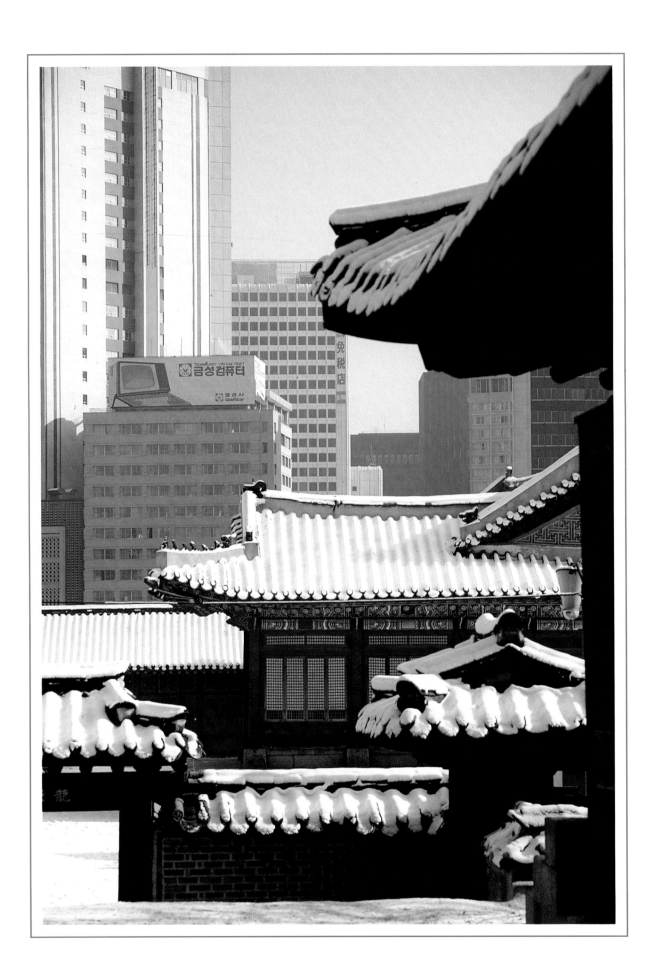

IN A CITY OF ANCIENT PALACES and tall modern buildings, of narrow, winding old streets and superhighways, of serene Buddhist temples and boisterous street markets, in an apartment on an island overlooking a river stands an eight-year-old girl thinking about a fish named Fatso. And about school tomorrow.

The city is Seoul. The country is the Republic of Korea. But most people call it simply South Korea. The river is the Han River. Yoido (yuh ee doh) is the name of the island. Kwang Chung is the name of the apartments, and Kim Chi-hoon is the name of the girl. Fish are mostly the same as anywhere. School, well, not exactly.

Korea is located on the eastern edge of Asia. The Korean peninsula extends southward from the point where Russia bumps into China. The other nearest neighbors are Japan and Taiwan. Korean geographers like to say that their land resembles a rabbit. The ears are up

north in the east. The tail sits down south, slightly off to the west of where it would be if the rabbit were drawn just right. The tail is a famous, beautiful part of Korea called Cheju-do (chay joo doh). It is another island.

Seoul, about thirty miles inland, is surrounded by mountains. When Seoul was first built, it stood on the north bank of the Han River. The river flowed outside a great wall that encircled the city. In the past twenty-five years, however, Seoul has grown so quickly that the city has expanded across the Han, and far beyond. The river now flows through the middle of the ever-growing city, which has ten million people.

Before the city expanded across the river, there was a sandbar in it. The sandbar was big enough to have a name: *Yoido* (*do* is the Korean word for "island"). Yoido became a landing strip for military airplanes. Seoul's first airport was there. Then an apartment building was built.

Then another, and another. Yoido became a bustling, exciting place to live. After building a grand National Assembly Building, the government moved its offices to Yoido. And among the many persons who live there now is the family of Kim Chi-hoon.

Kim Chi-hoon lives with her older sister, Kim Chi-young; with her parents, Kim Seung-kyung and Yu Young-nan; and with five fish. Chi-hoon, at eight, is two years younger than Chi-young. Kim is their family name. It comes from their father, Kim Seung-kyung. In Korea the family name is always written first.

The girls' mother is named Yu Young-nan; Korean women do not change their family names after marriage. Once a woman becomes a mother, everyone calls her by the name of her oldest child or her oldest son. Young-nan is called "Chi-young Omma."

Chi-hoon calls her mother Omma (uh-mah), which means "mommy." She calls her father Apa (op pa), the Korean word for "daddy." And she calls her sister Oni (uh nee). Oni is the name younger sisters in Korea must call their older sisters. Korean people believe in showing respect to those who are older. Chi-hoon also adds the word *Oni* to the names of girl friends or cousins who are older than she is.

All Korean children are expected to keep a diary. In the diary, or *Il Gi* (eel gee), the children write about school as well as life outside of school. The *Il Gi* is then presented to their teachers, who read it once a week.

Picking up her pencil, Chi-hoon thinks about yesterday and today — Saturday and Sunday. Outside her window she sees a brightly lit tour boat floating on the Han, and wonders what to write in her diary today. Then she writes:

토 요 일 (SATURDAY) *One fish died. His name was Fatso. Oni and her friend Kyong-min Oni picked the dead fish out of the aquarium. We buried him near the swings by our building. Oni said, "Let's sprinkle water over the grave when spring comes." The reason Fatso died was because we gave him too much food.*

일 요 일 (SUNDAY) *We went to Noryangjin Fish Market. Omma bought* urok *and* tomi, *two kinds of fish. She had the man slice the fish very pretty. For eating. I am sorry for the fish. I will never eat raw fish when I grow up. My Oni said it was gross.*

Chi-hoon feels sad about the fish her mother and father ate, and about Fatso, and because Chi-young was braver about picking Fatso out of the aquarium. Watching the boat move down the river, Chi-hoon wonders if the people on the boat are watching her. She quickly tires of feeling sad about fish. Tomorrow is Monday, and Monday is school. Monday is also the day for school prizes. *Perhaps*, Chi-hoon thinks, *this is the week I will win a prize.* That thought is enough to make her happy. Chi-hoon very much wants to win a school prize.

MONDAY

THE NEXT MORNING Chi-hoon stands with her class-mates in an untidy line outside of school. Every Monday morning, at every Korean school, the students gather outside for the weekly assembly called *Cho-hoe* (cho whay), which means "morning meeting." Children are running into the school yard so they will not be late. Stragglers are stopped by the yellow-helmeted crossing guards. The unlucky ones will miss assembly, and their names will be given to their teachers.

As Chi-hoon looks up and around from her place in line, she sees the apartment buildings of Yoido reaching up to the sky. Everywhere Chi-hoon looks, she sees more and more apartment buildings. Chi-hoon looks over at the principal's platform. Soon the principal will stand there and give the

students important words to think about this week. At the head of each line of students, the teachers stand and wait as well. This morning Chi-hoon thinks she might like to be a teacher someday and be in charge of all the children. If she were a teacher, she would change a few of the rules. Younger sisters in her class would not have to call older sisters Oni unless they wanted to. Each week one teacher would win a prize for

having the nicest dress. Chi-hoon thinks she would like to stand on the platform with the principal so she could see everything, too.

One of the teachers calls out, and the untidy lines quickly turn into neat, measured lines. Each student places a hand on the shoulder of the student in front and steps one arm length behind. Then, hands at their sides, the students sing the Korean national anthem, accompanied by a loud, scratchy record. Next, the school song is sung, without the aid of a loud, scratchy record. Voices rise loudly to the words:

In the middle of Seoul, near the Yoido Plaza,

Where the clear, clean water from Tae-bok Mountain flows,

And where, with the great will of the Korean people, we founded this school,

We grow as beautiful as flowers,

And our school shines as brightly as the morning star.

As the song finishes, Principal Lee bounds down the school stairs and up to the platform. He begins to talk of many things to his pupils. Chi-hoon wishes he would hurry up and announce the prizes.

"And today's prizes…"

Chi-hoon listens now. Principal Lee tells the students that the police station nearest the school is awarding this week's prizes to the three students who are the most dutiful and respectful. Before he announces the winners, Principal Lee wishes to remind all the students, but particularly the girls, of the story of Shim Chung.

Shim Chung? wonders Chi-hoon. She knows the story—everyone knows the story. It is one of the most famous of all Korean tales, told over and over. And now to be told again by Principal Lee.

"Shim Chung was the daughter of a poor blind man," he begins. "She was a good daughter, who knew that her most important responsibility was to care for and respect her father. She did everything she could for him.

"One day Shim Chung's father fell into a river and was rescued by a Buddhist monk. The monk told Shim Chung's father that if he brought three hundred bags of rice to the temple, he would regain his sight. Three hundred bags of rice? The monk might as well have asked for three hundred bags of gold. Shim Chung's father was a poor man with no rice to share.

"When Shim Chung's father told her of the monk's offer, she wished in her heart that she could help her father regain his sight. Soon, some sailors came to town. They wanted to sail to China but knew they could not make the voyage safely without offering a sacrifice to the sea dragon. The sailors wished to buy a young girl who would be the sacrifice. Shim Chung said she would go with the sailors if

they would give her three hundred bags of rice, delivered to the Buddhist temple. So the bargain was struck.

"Shim Chung took good care of her father until the very moment she left with the sailors. When a raging storm threatened the boat, Shim Chung leapt into the sea calling out to her father."

Principal Lee ends his story there, reminding the students of their responsibilities to their parents, to their school, and to their country. But Chi-hoon loves the rest of the story. Shim Chung did not drown but was carried away to the kingdom of the Sea King. The Sea King wanted Shim Chung to stay in his palace as his daughter. Shim Chung's heart was too heavy. She could think only of her poor father left behind. And Chi-hoon likes best when Shim Chung

leaves the palace under the sea in a lotus flower. Sailors find the flower and bring it ashore as a gift to the king. When the king's son sees Shim Chung, he falls immediately in love with her. Shim Chung marries him, becomes a princess, and is reunited with her father, who regains his sight. Chi-hoon wonders whether she would rather be a king's daughter under the sea or a princess above the sea.

Just then, Principal Lee announces the prize winners. Three names are called — three names that are not Kim Chi-hoon. Three students break the neat lines, bow to the teachers, and bow to Principal Lee as he gives them their prizes. The school's head student begins his speech, but Chi-hoon hardly listens. She is thinking how wonderful it would be to win a prize.

She is remembering how much she complained this morning when her Apa told her to carry some rubbish down with her on the elevator. And she is thinking of how cross she was with her Oni because Chi-young had a friend to walk to school with, while Chi-hoon had only the friend's brother. Chi-hoon worries that Shim Chung would not have done these things.

I want to win a prize, Chi-hoon decides. *I will try harder. All this week I will be the best daughter, the most dutiful daughter since Shim Chung. And then I will win next week's prize.*

All that day at school Chi-hoon tries to talk, sit, and even eat as dutifully as she can. On the way home from school, she stops at the stationery store to buy supplies she will need for music class. Usually Chi-hoon forgets to remind her mother that she needs supplies for the morning until late the night before. Shim Chung would never do that to her mother, if she had a mother.

Reaching home, Chi-hoon rushes inside. Of course, she takes off her shoes first. She would never wear shoes in her home or in any Korean home. That would be rude. In the past, Korean homes were heated from under the floor by a system call *ondol.* People sat on the floor cushions, ate at tables low to the ground, and slept on the floor —

all to be nearer the warmth. Shoes would bring outside dirt into the home; shoes might damage the floors, which were built thin to allow the heat to come through; and shoes would be a barrier between the warm floor and feet that were in need of warming. Today some Korean homes are heated by *ondol,* and some are not; but in all homes there is a place at the door for leaving shoes.

Chi-hoon goes to the fish tank first and carefully measures the food. A dutiful daughter would not kill fish by feeding them too much.

"Omma, Omma," Chi-hoon calls to her mother, who is working at the desk. Almost every day when Chi-hoon comes home from school, her mother is working at the computer. Yu Young-nan translates books from English into Korean. Today she is working on a biography. Chi-hoon tells her mother that she is going downstairs to ride her bicycle so Young-nan can work in quiet. Chi-hoon decides that Chi-young should go with her.

But Chi-young is reading a book. Chi-hoon thinks that Chi-young is *always* reading a book. "Oni, come play with me," Chi-hoon says.

"I'm reading," Chi-young says.

"You can stop now, Oni," Chi-hoon insists.

"After this chapter," Chi-young offers.

"Chi-young, now!" Chi-hoon stamps her foot and rushes from the apartment. Chi-hoon is cross with her Oni. She thinks Oni should help her younger sister be a good daughter by riding bicycles with her. As Chi-hoon rides the paths around Kwang Chung Apartments, she wonders how to ride a bicycle dutifully.

In her diary this evening, Chi-hoon writes:

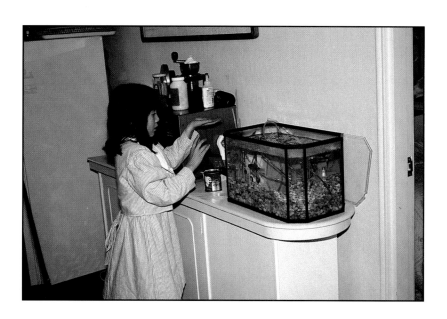

월요일 (MONDAY) *Today was the day for school prizes. I thought I might win. But I did not. I rode my bicycle alone till So-yon came. Then I was happy. Chi-young came later. Chi-hee also came to play. We all played "House" near Building Six and Building Seven.*

Chi-hoon thinks about how brave Shim Chung was to go with the sailors. Chi-hoon would like to be that brave. But if sailors came right now, up from the Han River, looking for a good daughter to sacrifice, Chi-hoon thinks she would not go. She would offer Chi-young instead.

TUESDAY

CHI-HOON TRIES HARD to concentrate in math class this morning. The monthly tests are coming soon. Adults are always asking Chi-hoon — always asking *all* the children—"How did you do on the last test?" Some teachers become very angry with their students who do badly, and they punish the students. Chi-hoon worries about the tests.

Today, Teacher Chung works problems on the blackboard. In the back of the room, two boys run up and hit two other boys on the head. Teacher Chung doesn't see them, but she hears the noise. She guesses who might have caused the trouble and speaks to the two boys, but they do not listen. Chi-hoon is quite sure those two boys will not win a prize this week.

Math is finally finished.

Lunch begins. Chi-hoon's class rushes down the stairs to the cafeteria. Not all Korean schools have cafeterias, but Chi-hoon's does. The students' parents are proud that their children go to a school with a cafeteria that offers a hot lunch every day. Mothers of the students take turns serving the food.

Along with her classmates, Chi-hoon picks up a sectioned metal tray, chopsticks, and a long spoon. Lunch today is *taktchim*

(tock jeem), which is a chicken stew; soup, which is served every day and today contains spinach and tofu; *pap* (bop), which is rice; *hobak* (hoe bock), which is a green vegetable something like a zucchini and something like a pumpkin; and *kimchi* (kimchee), which is one of the most important parts of a Korean meal.

Kimchi is a pickled, spiced vegetable (usually cabbage but sometimes radish or cucumber) that Koreans eat with every single meal. In the backyards of houses and on the balconies of apartments throughout Seoul are brown ceramic pots, both large and small, which hold each family's *kimchi*. There is even a time each fall called *kimchi* time. This used to be the time the women of the family made a year's supply of *kimchi*. The brown pots were buried in the ground where the cold would preserve them. Now that so many people have refrigerators, *kimchi* is often made all year round.

Today, as every day, the cafeteria is filled with loud noise. Chi-hoon sits with her friend So-yon. Sometimes So-yon comes to Chi-hoon's apartment to play. So-yon likes most to play hairdresser. Last week the two friends were bakers; with clay they made crescent cakes and rice cakes.

Glancing around the cafeteria, Chi-hoon sees her sister Chi-young sitting with a friend. She also sees their cousin Chi-min. Chi-min has a brother Chi-woo. Another cousin, Chi-hee, has lunch as well. Chi-hee has a new brother, Chi-sook. There is a good reason why the cousins' names are so alike. *Chi* is their generation name. Their grandfather chose this name to be the first name

of children born to his sons. Children born to his daughters receive their generation name from their father's father. A wise person called a *chom jaengi* (chum jang ee) is often consulted to choose a name which will bring the greatest good fortune.

When lunch is over, the students go back to the classroom. There is no outside exercise today; the students will study history, geography, and Korean language as well as music and art.

After school today, Chi-young sits in the living room reading a book. Chi-hoon sits on the kitchen floor and helps Ajuma make *kkwabaeji* (kwah beh jee). Ajuma comes to the house three mornings a week to help Young-nan with cooking and cleaning. *Ajuma* is the Korean word used to address an older woman who is not a member of the family, especially a woman who comes to help with cooking and cleaning. Chi-hoon likes Ajuma very much. She is always happy to see her and happiest when Ajuma makes cookies.

Ajuma is very good at

making *kkwabaeji*. These cookies are tricky to make because the dough has to be rolled very thin and then sliced just right. Chi-hoon's job is to join the ends together and then turn the circles inside out, making the *kkwabaeji* shape. Chi-hoon believes that helping Ajuma make cookies shows that she is a dutiful daughter.

The cookies finished, Chi-hoon carries in drinks for Omma, Oni, and herself. A *kkwabaeji* party! Chi-hoon waits while Chi-young reads the school paper. Once a week a newspaper is delivered to school. The paper looks just like a newspaper that adults read, but it is for children. The newspaper has stories, comics, news articles, and projects to make. Chi-hoon shares the paper with her Oni, but Chi-hoon always wants to read it first. Because she complains so loudly and makes such sad faces, Chi-young always gives in.

But Chi-hoon worries about this today. She thinks that Shim Chung would never have wanted to sacrifice her sister to a sea monster. So today she waits while Chi-young reads the paper first. Still, Chi-hoon bounces from side to side to see if that hurries Chi-young along.

After the *kkwabaeji* party, Chi-hoon goes to her piano lesson. On the way, she sees Chonyondong (chun yun dong) Grandmother's car outside the apartment building of Changun Omma (jah geun uh mah). *Changun Omma*—"Little Mother"—is what Chi-hoon calls her youngest uncle's wife. Changun Omma is the mother of Chihee and Chi-sook. Chi-hoon says "Chonyondong Grandmother" to distinguish her father's mother from her mother's mother. Most Korean children call their father's parents *halmoni* (hahl mun nee), which means "grandmother," and *haraboji* (hah rah bud gee), which means "grandfather." Their mother's parents are called *oe halmoni* (weh hahl mun nee) and *oe haraboji* (weh hah rah bud gee), which mean "outside grandmother" and "outside grandfather." Traditionally, the mother's parents were not thought to be as important as the father's parents. But Chi-hoon, Chi-young, and their parents do not think this is fair. So they call Seung-kyung's parents Chonyondong Grandmother and Grandfather because Chonyondong is the part of Seoul where these grandparents live. Young-nan's parents are called Seoul Apartment Grandmother and Grandfather because they live in an apartment building of that name.

At piano lessons Chi-hoon tries to pay attention and concentrate. Usually she tries to play with her friends who are there for lessons

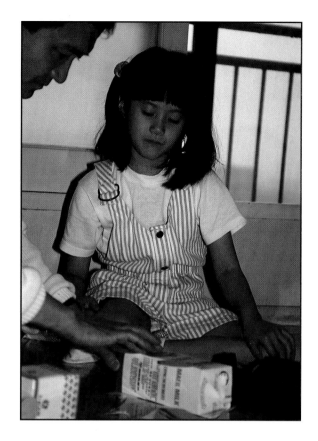

also. Today Chi-hoon laughs only three times when she is playing. Usually she laughs the whole time. Shim Chung would have only laughed once, Chi-hoon thinks—that is, if Shim Chung had had piano lessons, which she didn't, because her father was poor.

When she returns home after her lessons, Chi-hoon sees the big bunch of garlic that Chonyondong Grandmother has brought over. The garlic is so tall that Chi-hoon picks it up to dance with it. She dances the garlic to the kitchen for Young-nan to hang.

That night Chi-hoon's father helps her with her school assignment. Most Korean fathers work very long hours; Seung-kyung works long hours at a bank. But he tries very hard to spend time with Chi-hoon and Chi-young and help them with their homework.

This evening, Chi-hoon and her father are building a truck out of milk cartons.

"Why are we building a truck?" Seung-kyung wonders out loud as he helps Chi-hoon attach the wheels.

"Because that is the assignment," Chi-hoon says. Chi-hoon is sure that the students who win prizes are those who complete their assignments. While the glue dries on the truck, Chi-hoon takes out her diary and writes:

화요일 (TUESDAY) *I am happy today. All day I was as good as Shim Chung. If the prize were given today, I would win. I did not even tell So-yon that she was wrong when she said Miss Korea was beautiful. I think Miss Korea has ugly hair.*

WEDNESDAY

ALMOST LATE. Chi-hoon races into the school yard, trying to catch up with her schoolmates. She is late because she stopped to talk with Changun Omma, who was walking her baby, Chi-sook. The school is just a few short blocks from Kwang Chung Apartments, so Chi-hoon makes it just in time. Chi-hoon knows that students do not win prizes by being late for school.

Inside the classroom, she carefully places the milk-carton truck on the shelf under the straw painting she made last week.

"Music class!" announces Teacher Chung as she pushes and shoves the great drum to the middle of the room. Happily, Chi-hoon takes her tambourine out of its special tambourine case. Music is surely the easiest class in which to be good.

The class first practices rhythmic timing and clapping. *Bang, bang, thump, thump* goes the big drum as the teacher hits it with all her might. *Clang, clang, thrum, thrum* go the tambourines softly. Then the class sings "The Paper-Folding Song." Paper folding is called *chon-gi chop-ki* (chohng ee jup kee) in Korea. Most people elsewhere know paper folding by the Japanese word *origami*. All the students sing the words as loudly as they can, banging their tambourines in time:

What shall I fold with my red
 red paper?
What shall I fold with my blue
 blue paper?
I shall make a pretty flower with
 red red paper.
And with blue blue paper I will
 fold a pretty pretty bird.
Bloom red flowers in a green field,
 Blue blue birds fly in the blue sky.

The teacher then selects three boys and three girls to do a special dance to the paper-folding song while the other children sing along. The students are asked to clap for the best dancer. Chi-hoon wonders whether she should clap for the girl she likes best or for the girl who dances best. Chi-hoon decides

to vote for the girl who was her best friend last month.

After school is finished, Chi-hoon must stay longer than usual, so she cannot walk home with her Oni. Today Chi-hoon is on the classroom cleaning team. In Chi-hoon's school the children are responsible for cleaning the classroom, the halls, and the bathrooms. Chi-hoon's friend Sung-un is in the same cleaning group, so Chi-hoon does not mind staying late. As they push the big brooms back and forth across the classroom, the two friends sing the paper-folding song.

When Chi-hoon arrives home, Youngnan tells her to hurry and change so they can go to the market. Chi-young has to go to a math class, so Chi-hoon will have her Omma

with their tests so they will be able to attend a good university someday.

Quite close to Kwang Chung Apartments is a supermarket, which does not look too different from a supermarket in other countries. Young-nan does much of her shopping there. But she also shops in the traditional markets found all over Seoul. Some of these markets are huge — covering great city blocks — and some are small, like the one where they are headed now. Korean markets are wonderful, crowded jumbles. People sell grains, rice, umbrellas, fish so fresh they're still swimming, eggs, chickens, toys, meat, bread, shoes — anything and everything.

Young-nan and Chi-hoon buy *ttalgi* (dahl

all to herself. Chi-young takes just one class, but most of her friends take more than one class. They study math, computers, and English, among other subjects. Their parents hope all the extra study will help them

moni both tried to be good daughters. And she wonders if it was easy for them.

Back home again, Chi-hoon learns that Komo called while they were out. *Komo* is another Korean word for "aunt," but it only means a sister of your father. Chi-hoon and Chi-young like their Komo very much. She phoned to see if the girls would go with her tomorrow to the Buddhist temple.

"No thank you," says Chi-young, who knows she doesn't want to go.

"I'll go," says Chi-hoon, who isn't sure if she wants to go but thinks she might be more like Shim Chung if she does something she does not want to do. Just before going to bed, Chi-hoon writes:

수요일 (WEDNESDAY) *After lunch we had a painting contest. There were two titles. One was to draw an unpolluted house. The other was to draw our neighborhood playground. I drew the playground. Most children drew the playground. I do not know who won. I will see Komo tomorrow. Then I will be happy.*

kee), *pae* (peh), *chamoe* (chahm weh), and a ball with pink sparkles. *Ttalgi* are strawberries. *Pae* is something like an apple and something like a pear, but better than both. *Chamoe* are small, sweet yellow melons. And the ball with pink sparkles is just that.

As Chi-hoon and her mother walk, Chi-hoon remembers her father telling how he loved to walk to the market with his Omma when he was a boy. Chi-hoon wonders if Chonyondong Grandmother liked to walk to market with her mother. Grandmother's mother is called Kun Halmoni, which means "Big Grandmother," even though she is very small and quite old. She still comes to dinner every Saturday night. Chi-hoon wonders if Chonyondong Grandmother and Kun Hal-

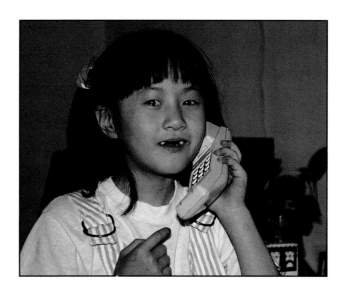

THURSDAY

ROM THE BACK of Komo's car, Chi-hoon watches what seem to be millions and millions of cars trying to squeeze into the narrow streets of Seoul. Everywhere she looks there are cars, cars, cars, buses, buses, and more cars. The streets of Seoul must be the busiest streets in the whole world. That, at least, is what Chi-hoon thinks.

They drive past Namdaemun (nahm deh moon), which is the Korean National Treasure Number One. *Mun* means "gate." *Namdaemun* means "Great South Gate," which was also once called the Gate of Exalted Ceremony. This was long ago, when a massive wall encircled all of Seoul. King Taejo had the wall built in 1396, not long after the founding of Seoul. Almost two hundred thousand men came from all over Korea to build the wall. The only way in, or out, of the city was through the gates. A great bell rang out at sunset to warn everyone that the gates would soon close for the

evening. A bell rang again in the early morning to signal the opening of the gates. Today one of these bells can be found in a beautiful,

painted belfry on the corner of Chong-no. And what does *Chong-no* mean? "Bell Street."

At Pomun-sa (poe moon sah) Chi-hoon, Komo, and her cousin Son-woo enter through the temple gate. *Sa* is the Korean word for "temple." As a Buddhist, Komo has arranged for a special ceremony today. During the ceremony she will pray that her children will have success in preparing for and taking their tests. Any student who wishes to attend a university in Korea must take the nationwide college test. These tests are extremely difficult. The students with the highest scores go to the best schools. Everyone worries about these all-important tests. Komo's family will not take the time even to come to Chonyondong Grandparents' house for dinner for one whole year so

done in a specific order. Chi-hoon watches Komo and tries to do it exactly right. Once, Chi-hoon cannot help herself; she giggles when she gets it wrong. So she tries hard to think only good and useful thoughts. She thinks of her cousins studying so hard for their tests. She thinks how she does not like studying as often as she has to. She thinks of Komo, who is so nice and so worried. Mostly Chi-hoon thinks that her Oni was right. Chi-hoon's knees hurt.

that the studying can go on uninterrupted.

Chi-hoon follows Komo and her cousin as they walk up the high hill to the grotto at the back of the temple grounds. In front of the massive statue of Buddha, they will pray for the success of Komo's children. Komo, Chi-hoon, and Son-woo light incense sticks at the foot of the grotto, remove their shoes, and then step up toward the statue.

Chi-hoon meets the Buddhist nun who will lead the ceremony. They all kneel on cushions before the great statue of Buddha. The nun chants as they kneel and listen. Now and then she bangs a wooden gong. Then they must all perform a complicated ritual bow, over and over again, until she signals them to stop. The bow clears their minds of other thoughts and helps them focus on the ceremony. At least, it is supposed to do that. The bowing is difficult and must be

목요일 (THURSDAY) *I went to Pomun-sa with Komo and Son-woo. The temple was interesting. The wood gong made a lovely sound. The kneeling was not so good. I pretended I was Shim Chung. I asked Buddha for long golden hair.*

OUTSIDE Chi-young's classroom, Chi-hoon jumps from foot to foot. Waiting. Today is the day Chi-young has to clean her classroom. Chi-hoon can see her Oni washing the blackboard with a big yellow sponge. Today is also the day that Omma told Chi-hoon and Chi-young she would take them on an outing. The biography is translated, and Young-nan has promised they will go to Kyongbuk-kung (kyung bohk koong) to practice drawing. Kyongbuk-kung! This is one of Chi-hoon's and Chi-young's favorite places in Seoul. *Kung* is a "palace"; *Kyongbuk-kung* is the "Palace of Shining Happiness." It is one of the most beautiful spots in all of Seoul and, in a most crowded city, one of the nicest for walking.

Kyongbuk-kung is not one building but a great space sur-

rounded by a wall and filled with buildings. At one time there were more than five hundred. Today there are about fifty. The palace buildings were home to the king and queen, their children, and the many members of the extended royal family. A vast army of servants took care of life in the palace. The offices of the government were in Kyongbuk-kung; the throne room was here as well as places for the learned men of the day to meet. Kyongbuk-kung had many

gardens, several ponds, and a vast courtyard where the soldiers of the king would assemble.

No one lives in Kyongbuk-kung any more. The last member of the Korean royal family who lived in one of the palaces died in 1988. The palace is now a place for learning how the long-ago kings lived and ruled, a place for walking, and a place for visiting two buildings that house museums.

Any time that there are people in Kyongbuk-kung, there is surely someone drawing or painting. Drawing and painting are considered important parts of education in Korea. All Korean schoolchildren have sketchbooks, drawing pencils, and watercolor paints, which they use frequently. Classes take trips to Kyongbuk-kung and other scenic sights in Seoul just to paint them. On weekends the palace is filled with people, young and old, sitting where they can, painting the beauty they see.

When they enter Kyongbuk-kung, Chi-hoon insists on going straight to Hyang-won-jung (hyang on jung). This is the Pavilion of Far Reaching Fragrance. The pavilion sits in the center of a lotus pond. A lovely arched bridge leads across the pond. Chi-hoon likes to imagine she is the queen, dressed in the finest court dress, walking across the bridge.

The two sisters sit a while sketching the pavilion. Chi-hoon cannot sit too long. "Omma, Omma," she says, "I want to go to Kunjong-jon (koun jung jun)." This is the throne room of the palace. On the stone platform that surrounds the throne hall are wonderful carvings of mythical creatures and the signs of the zodiac.

Korean people believe that each year is represented by an animal. Each year's animal sign is very important to the people who were born under it. Seung-kyung, Chi-hoon's father, was born in the year of the dragon. Young-nan was born in the year of the monkey, and Chi-young in the year of the *toegi* (toak kee)—or "rabbit." Chi-hoon was born in the year of the *twaeji* (dweh jee), the year of the pig. She has always been unhappy that she was born in that year. She wishes her year had a nicer animal, like a dog, or an exciting animal, like a tiger. Chi-hoon often says she was born in the year of the koala bear instead of the year of the pig.

Today, the girls search the platform carvings to find a dragon, a monkey, a rabbit, and a pig. They find the first three carvings but no pig. Chi-hoon calls to Chi-young that she has found a koala bear. Chi-young says there are no koala bear carvings in Kyongbuk-kung and no year of the koala bear. Chi-hoon thinks there is, and if she were a queen, she would make a royal decree doing away with the year of the pig.

While Young-nan walks to a re-freshment stand, Chi-hoon and Chi-young sit swinging their legs on a bench.

"This is my favorite place," Chi-hoon says.

"I like the folk village a little better," Chi-young says.

"I think I like them both exactly the same," Chi-hoon answers.

The sisters are remembering the day, just a few weeks ago, when their parents took them to the Korean folk village a little way outside Seoul. The folk village recreates Korean life as it was lived in past times. Chi-young remembers feeding a goat. Chi-hoon remembers the tightrope walker who she thinks must be the best tightrope walker ever, any-where. They both re-member the farmers' dance, which was very fast and very loud.

Sitting on the bench

in the sun, Chi-hoon thinks she was not as good a daughter that day as she is today. There is a place in the folk village that sells hamburgers for lunch. Hamburgers are not really a meal from Korea's past, but Chi-hoon wanted one. Her father wanted the family to go together for *pibimpap* (pee beem bop). *Pibimpap* is a meal of rice and vegetables, served in a heavy stone bowl. A *pibimpap* bowl looks like it could hold a witch's brew. But it is not a hamburger,

afternoon. They see three brides having pictures taken on the grass. They see a man whose job it is to keep the brides off the grass. He never wins. They see a Boy Scout troop. A group of giggling teenage girls walks by; each girl has a sketch pad under her arm. They see a tour guide holding a flag aloft, followed by a large group of visitors from Japan.

which is what Chi-hoon wanted. So she sulked a little, and she knows Shim Chung would not have.

Young-nan brings the cool drinks, and all three of them sit watching the other people who have come to Kyongbuk-kung this

Chi-hoon sees a small red-haired boy walking with his mother. The mother is wearing cowboy boots, so the girls decide she must be an American. Chi-hoon and Chi-young see the whole group of giggling art students surround the red-haired boy

and his mother. Everyone takes the boy's picture. And a busload of grandmothers comes to see the palace. They are all wearing the same kind of yellow baseball caps.

Later Chi-hoon and her sister and mother leave the palace through a beautiful gate in the wall. Ancient Kyongbuk-kung is surrounded by the modern skyscrapers of Seoul. The three go from a peaceful palace into horrible traffic. That's Seoul.

In her diary tonight, Chi-hoon tapes the entry ticket from the palace. She enjoys putting mementos, not just words, in her *Il Gi*. One time Chi-hoon wrote about some dead ants she found. She stuck the dead ants to some tape which she stuck inside the diary. While looking to see if the ants are still there, Chi-hoon reads about the time her whole class went to Kyongbuk-kung.

수요일 (WEDNESDAY) *We went on a school picnic. We went to Kyongbuk-kung. After lunch it rained. First the boys had their pictures taken together. Then the girls. Because of the rain, we couldn't play games. Instead, we sang and told riddles on the bus. It was fun.*

Turning the pages to the most recent entry, Chi-hoon writes:

금요일 (FRIDAY) *We went to Kyongbuk-kung. Omma, Oni, and I. We made pictures and we walked. I ate a banana. More and more I think I am like Shim Chung. But I should have let Oni pick where to draw. I did not today. But I was happy.*

SATURDAY

SCHOOL AGAIN TODAY. The bad part of Saturday, Chi-hoon thinks, is having to go to school, even for a half day. Even though Chi-hoon has always gone to school for a half day on Saturday, she thinks it should be a day to play instead. The good part of Saturday is that her father works only half a day. Chi-hoon and Chi-young love Saturday afternoons with their Apa. Sometimes they bicycle on Yoido Plaza, a huge open space in front of the National Assembly. Sometimes they go for hikes or on special outings—like their trip to the folk village.

And today? "Tennis, tennis!" is what the sisters want to play. And always, on Saturdays, they go to dinner with their father's family at Chonyondong Grandparents' house.

The tennis courts are a short walk from their apartment through the streets of Yoido.

Chi-hoon loves to play tennis. She would really like to play it well. But she finds it too easy to miss the ball, and easier to laugh.

"Chi-young hits the ball because she pays attention. Now you try watching the ball," Seung-kyung says as he tries to teach his second daughter.

I will watch, thinks Chi-hoon, as she swings and misses. Every time she misses, Chi-hoon laughs so hard that she misses the next ball as well. *What a good game this is,*

him in person. Grand-mother is hardly in the kitchen today; she is too busy holding the baby Chi-sook. Chi-hoon tells Grand-mother she would like to hold him. "You should talk to your mother, Chi-hoon," Grandmother says as she bounces Chi-sook up and down. Chi-hoon doesn't say anything.

Chi-hoon thinks, as she happily swings and misses.

Then on to Chonyondong for dinner. Chi-hoon is always glad to come to Chon-yondong. Even though her grandfather calls her every day at home to ask about school and her marks on the tests, it is nicer to see

Chi-hoon's aunts and mother serve dinner to Grandfather, Grandmother, Great-Grandmother, Seung-kyung, and all the children. The family sits on floor cushions, eating from a low table. At family dinners, or at any special dinner in Korea, there is a parade of dishes. They are placed in the center of the table. Every-

one eats from them with chop-sticks—except for the rice. Everyone gets a separate small bowl of rice.

After the grand-parents, the men, and the children eat, Young-nan, Kun Omma, and Changun Omma come into the room to eat. Chi-hoon and Chi-young know their mother does not like this. But this is the way it has always been done in Korea and the way it is still done in many people's homes. And this is the way it is done in Chonyon-dong Grandparents' home.

After dinner, all the girls try to hold Chi-sook. Chi-young wants to carry him on her back. Chi-hoon wants to sit and sing with him. Chi-hoon's grandfather points to the new baby. As Young-nan sits eating, he tells her, "You should have another baby. You need to have a boy." Chi-hoon watches her mother's face. She sees her mother become upset with this baby boy talk.

In the past, Korean people believed that it was much, much better for a baby to be a boy than a girl. They believed girls would only grow up, marry, and leave the family. Boys were responsible for taking care of their parents in their old age and bringing honor to the family. They thought a girl would be unable to do this. Some people in Korea still believe it is important for all families to have a son. Many others believe this idea is not a good one. Chonyondong Grandparents believe Chi-hoon's parents must have a son. Seung-kyung and Young-nan don't believe this. They are happy with their two daughters and do not want to change anything.

Because Chi-hoon and Chi-young love their parents and their grandparents, this talk of boy babies is hard to listen to. Chi-hoon just wishes it would go away. But she doesn't want Chi-sook to go away. She just wants to hold him. And tonight Chi-hoon writes:

토요일 (SATURDAY) *I played tennis. Sometimes I hit the ball. We went to Chonyondong. I was sad that Komo was not there. We watched television. We had bulgoki beef, salad, rice, hot beef soup, and kimchi.*

SUNDAY

RAINING! Chi-hoon stares at the rain. It is so heavy she can barely see the building just across the way. The rain annoys her. Seoul Apartment Grandfather was going to take them hiking at Namhan Sansong (nahm hahn san song). Chi-hoon wanted to go so badly. Namhan Sansong means "South Korean Mountain Fortress."

Long ago, a Korean king whose name was King Injo built a fortress as a place of escape in case Seoul were attacked. Twelve years after it was built, King Injo and over 12,000 soldiers ran to Namhan Sansong with a Chinese Manchu army right behind them. The plan was a good one, and might have worked, but they forgot to bring food for that many people and had to surrender when they got too hungry.

But there will be no going to Namhan Sansong today. Looking out at the Han River, Chi-hoon crosses her arms and makes a face at the river. *Sea monster weather,* she thinks. *Well, I wouldn't jump in the river today for all the rice in Korea.*

With rain whipping about them and a cold wind blowing, Chi-hoon's family drives the few short blocks to the Seoul Apartments. Komo and her family also live here,

Because of the wind and the rain, Chi-hoon's grandparents decide they should stay in and play Yut (yoot). Chi-hoon can hardly stand still while Young-nan fixes her *hanbok*. Chi-hoon loves to play Yut; she especially loves to win. Yut is a game people have been playing for so long that no one is quite sure when it began. Four sticks, lines etched on one side, smooth on the other, are thrown into the air. Points are scored depending on which way the sticks land.

After Yut, Seoul Apartment Grandmother suggests they practice their deep bows. Koreans bow hello to each other many times each day. During the year, there are times, such as Chusok and New Year's, when both children and adults must make special deep bows to their parents and grandparents. It is important, especially for a girl, to make the bows correctly. Today Chi-hoon doesn't mind.

Grandfather decides they will all go out for *kalbi* (kahl bee). Because of the rain, the *hanbok* are not worn. Grandfather's favorite restaurant is a village of small houses climbing the side of a hill. Each group of diners has its own house to eat in.

The waitress brings *pori-cha* (poe ree chah), a tea made from barley which is always served in Korean restaurants. Chi-hoon wants a soda instead. Chi-hoon's Apa tells her the tea is a better choice today. But Seoul Apartment Grandfather gets Chi-hoon a cola.

As at Chonyondong, there are lots of

but Chi-hoon knows she cannot visit them. Everyone at Komo's house is studying, or helping someone who is studying, or being quiet while someone studies.

Seoul Apartment Grandparents are wearing *hanbok* (hahn boak) this morning. "Please," the sisters ask their grandmother, who always says, "yes." She keeps *hanbok* for the girls to wear. *Hanbok* is the traditional Korean clothing. Not very long ago, everyone in Korea wore *hanbok* every day. Some older people, like Kun Halmoni, still wear it every day. And nearly all Korean people wear *hanbok* sometime during the year, perhaps at a wedding or at a boy's first birthday party or on special holidays.

dishes here: *kimchi*, rice, green salad, radish salad, soup, garlic, and more. After every special meal in Korea, noodles are served. Chi-hoon wants *nangmyon* (nang mee on), a famous cold noodle soup. Young-nan tells her it is too cold to eat *nangmyon*. But Grandfather orders it for her. Like grandfathers and grandmothers everywhere, Chi-hoon's grandparents like to spoil their grandchildren.

At home this Sunday night, Chi-hoon wonders what to write. She finds it difficult to think about today; all her thoughts are on tomorrow. She imagines Principal Lee reminding everyone how he spoke of Shim Chung at last week's assembly. He tells them that there will be only one prize today, a prize for a girl who is the most like Shim Chung—a girl who says hello politely, who

waits patiently for her turn to read the newspaper, who only laughs once at piano lessons, and who does not say that Miss Korea's hair is ugly. Then Principal Lee will call out, "Kim Chi-hoon."

"Chi-hoon," calls Oni, "finish writing and come play." So Chi-hoon writes:

일요일 (SUNDAY) *Today was the day we did not go to Namhan Sansong. I was not so sad because I won Yut. We went to Daewongak for lunch. We had kalbi. I was happy to have a cola and cold noodles so I didn't mind the rain. Oni and I practiced bowing so I am ready for New Year's.*

Chi-hoon and her Oni sit by the window and play the clapping game. Chi-hoon

wonders if Chi-young has noticed how good, how dutiful, her younger sister has been this week. Chi-hoon mentions the *Cho-hye*, the Monday meeting.

"Do you know Chung Yeon-hee, the one who won the prize last week?" Chi-hoon asks as they play. All the while, clap up, clap down, go hands fast .

Chi-young says, "No, but I see her walking to school."

"I think the prizes will be a big surprise tomorrow," Chi-hoon hints.

"I wonder who will win," says Chi-young.

"I think I know," says Chi-hoon. Clap, slap, clap.

"Teacher Cha says tomorrow's prize will be for the best runner. Yu Kyung-hee should win." says Chi-young.

Clap, slap. "What!" cries Chi-hoon.

❖   ❖   ❖

On a rainy Sunday, in an apartment overlooking a rain-filled river stands an eight-year-old girl. She is thinking about Shim Chung. And about dutiful daughters. Tomorrow morning Principal Lee will not call out the name of Kim Chi-hoon. She knows that now. Chi-hoon thinks Shim Chung would have been happy just to be a good daughter—prize or no. And Chi-hoon? She isn't so sure.

At a window in Yoido, a young girl looks out over the city of Seoul. She decides to practice running after school tomorrow. Chi-hoon is certain that someday soon there will be a prize for the most dutiful runner. She smiles. Chi-hoon will win that prize.